I0086976

ADVENTURES IN
PROPERTY MANAGEMENT

CHELSEA WERNER-JATZKE

SIBLING RIVALRY PRESS
LITTLE ROCK, ARKANSAS
DISTURB / ENRAPTURE

Adventures in Property Management
Copyright © 2017 by Chelsea Werner-Jatzke

Cover art by Joe Rudko
Cover design by Shaun Kardinal
Author photograph by Daniel Carrillo

All rights reserved. No part of this book may be reproduced or republished without written consent from the publisher, except by reviewers who may quote brief excerpts in connection with a review in a newspaper, magazine, or electronic publication; nor may any part of this book be reproduced, stored in a retrieval system, or transmitted in any form, or by any means be recorded without written consent of the publisher.

Sibling Rivalry Press, LLC
PO Box 26147
Little Rock, AR 72221

info@siblingrivalrypress.com

www.siblingrivalrypress.com

ISBN: 978-1-943977-26-0

This title is housed permanently in the Rare Books and Special Collections Vault of the Library of Congress.

First Sibling Rivalry Press Edition, January 2017

For my father, the first property manager

ADVENTURES IN
PROPERTY MANAGEMENT

TABLE OF
CONTENTS

EVERY ARRANGEMENT

One on top of the other, two women move into the building in two separate months. When the one woman moves in upstairs, a month after the other woman moves in downstairs, the audio of arrangement fills the downstairs unit. It sounds like splinters. Also, change.

This is the soundtrack of singledom: pushing the dresser into the bedroom, pulling the dining table into the living room, lugging the bookcases to the walls, the boxes of books to the bookcases. Upstairs, Upstairs Woman is all overhead lights and motivational music. It is her first time moving on her own, moving somewhere where she lives alone. She has been at it all day and into the night and is sweating and singing along with a song that never felt so important: yes, you *can* go your own way.

Downstairs, Downstairs Woman can't make her broom heard over the furniture scraping the hardwood floors above—though she knocks the broom handle against the ceiling and shakes her fist in the air and knocks the broom handle to the ceiling again and again until a bit of plaster flakes into her eye. She feels herself much too young to have plaster in her eye from shaking her fist in the air at something she can't see.

Downstairs Woman calls the onsite manager and insists she go upstairs and complain on her behalf.

"Plaster is falling from my ceiling, that's how bad it's been." Downstairs Woman, so irate.

The manager knocks on Upstairs Woman's door.

"Are you moving furniture?"

"Yes"

"Because it sounds like you are moving furniture."

"Yes"

"Could you not? It's 2 A.M."

"I'm almost done if you'll just help me with the couch."

And as they fit the couch a safe distance from the radiator by the door to the kitchen, the landlord hears the broom handle knocking from downstairs. Downstairs Woman standing in front of her couch, her couch arranged directly below the couch of Upstairs Woman. Upstairs, the manager stands in the exact same place in front of the couch, in the exact same place, and looks at the kitchen table in the exact same place as downstairs. The knocking continues and the landlord hears a bit of plaster dislodge from the ceiling downstairs and hears Downstairs Woman cursing and imagines her shaking her fist at the ceiling though the noise has stopped.

"Can you ask the woman downstairs to stop knocking on the ceiling like that? It's 2 A.M." Upstairs Woman, all indignation. "Yes, I will let her know." The manager, most insincere.

Upstairs and downstairs, women go to bed. As Downstairs Woman begins to feel something like relief, she thinks about the deadbolt. And she sits upright and places her feet on the floor at the side of the bed and she hears Upstairs Woman's feet touch down on the floorboards above her. And Downstairs Woman hears the creak of floorboards across the ceiling move in the same line she is walking from bedroom to living room to front door and back again. And Downstairs Woman hears Upstairs Woman get back into bed, a bed whose frame creaks under her pressure, above her own bed whose frame creaks under her pressure as she gets back in bed, and Downstairs Woman wonders if Upstairs Woman is naked too.

They never meet. Not in the hall, not at the mailboxes, they never handle each other's freshly washed drawers, impatient and emptying drying machines to finish their own loads. They both keep their phones on vibrate and their schedules coordinate, their alarms keeping each other on time, buzzing through the walls and floors of their bedrooms. They begin to exhibit each other's hand gestures and vocal inflections and only the onsite manager notices. They are aware of each other the way they are aware of the boiler in the basement; through the clicks and bangs echoing through the radiators.

To: Admin@metmgmt.net
Subject: Work Order
1/3/13

I think we have some wiring issues in the back staircase.
Also, the parking lot light bulb has burned out again.
Thanks in advance for sending someone out to fix.

ALL FIELDS MUST BE COMPLETED FOR CONSIDERATION OF APPROVAL BY MANAGEMENT

Building Name: Malden
Unit #: Back Stairs
Permission to Enter: ☒ Yes (quickest option)
　　　　　　　　　　　　☐ No (please schedule an appointment)
Pet(s): ☐ Yes
　　　　☒ No
*If pets are present & maintenance cannot enter due to pets, a $75 administrative fee will be applied

　☐ Priority 1 - Emergency! - No hot or cold water, heat or electricity, or a condition which is imminently hazardous to life

　☐ Priority 2 - High Priority - Repair to a major appliance (range/oven, refrigerator) or a major plumbing issue

　☒ Priority 3 - Standard repair - all other repairs

DESCRIPTION OF WORK

There are a number of bulbs out in the back staircase of the building and at the very bottom of the staircase in the basement. I tried changing bulbs and, nothing. I have searched for the fuse that I suspect is responsible and there isn't anything corresponding to these sockets.

The outside building light on the West side by parking lot is burnt out. Please replace.

(Signature) _____
(Date) _____1.3.13_____

HOUSEBROKEN

No one knows this dog. The last newcomer asks the new newcomer the question they were asked when they passed in the hall: Do you know this dog? Coming in or going out the answer is no. But they linger in the hall with this dog and their neighbors and the group grows and this dog wags its tail and this is the freedom of danger without consequences—this well-trained stray that nobody knows.

No one has any suggestions what to do with this dog besides feed it. So someone brings out some kibble and some wine and everyone tells a story. About Los Angeles where people dump pets, unwanted or uncared for, in buildings that they know are pet friendly. About the last cat they had and how it found them. About the turtle they freed in a P-patch in Manhattan when their roommate neglected it. About this well-groomed dog that nobody knows and maybe it got lost.

Then it's all, who knows more of the neighborhood dogs? And then they are listing all the neighborhood dogs. At first it's a competition but finally, it's a commentary on the neighborhood and yes, the owner of the brindled pit and the tan bulldog's walker and which is more do-able. Everyone follows the logic that the dog walker is more do-able because of the lower risk of running into each other every day, and what's so wrong with the familiar is that it's boring. A number of the neighbors are high-fiving. Then someone enters the building and doesn't know this dog.

Then someone calls the manager and she comes down with a bottle of wine and says, Isaac? and the dog looks at her and wags its tail. Then someone says, Lucy! and the dog looks at them and wags its tail. And each person in the growing group starts in with Lucky, Shooter, Patch, Tiger, Titus, Flipper! Flipper? Yeah,

Flipper. Madison, Honey, Lucifer, Beyoncé, Prince. And someone brings out a boom box with their cassette tape of *Purple Rain* and the dog is spinning around the entryway of the building between people though no one is calling out to it and never was since no one knows this dog.

The tenants bring their own dogs out and prop open the side door, spilling into the parking lot. There are nine dogs and twelve beers and the cigarette smoke is drifting into the building and when someone inside complains the manager asks them if they want a dog. No, no one wants this dog—this wild beast pooping in the parking lot. So the manager says, "Maybe I will have a dog?" And she imagines this, this animal and her, an animal.

A window cracks on the third floor and the voice from it can hardly be heard and Prince yells back, *my luck's gonna change tonight / there's gotta be a better life* and the group toasts the building and invites the voice down, hoping for another joiner. The woman from 301 comes down and the manager thinks it can't be, someone should have known a dog that's lived in the building for four years, collar or no. She hopes that 301 is just coming down for a beer and that microchips are for the birds and the birds don't mind—pay attention, they call—this is how one migrates, this is how one flies.

This dog sees his owner and the potential of the unknown hits a pitch and Prince hits a high note and the last beer is knocked over by Isaac's tail as he rushes upstairs to his apartment. Prince is still playing and everyone feels stupid. No one recognized this dog but everyone recognized his comfort in a collar.

To: Admin@metmgmt.net
Subject: Work Order Follow-Up
2/13/13

I put in the work order for this... I can't even remember when. Any idea when someone will be out to fix?

ALL FIELDS MUST BE COMPLETED FOR CONSIDERATION OF APPROVAL BY MANAGEMENT

Building Name: Malden
Unit #: Back Stairs
Permission to Enter: **X** Yes (quickest option)
                           ☐ No (please schedule an appointment)
Pet(s):   ☐ Yes
            X No
*If pets are present & maintenance cannot enter due to pets, a $75 administrative fee will be applied

☐   Priority 1 - Emergency! - No hot or cold water, heat or electricity, or a condition which is imminently hazardous to life

☐   Priority 2 - High Priority - Repair to a major appliance (range/oven, refrigerator) or a major plumbing issue

X   Priority 3 - Standard repair - all other repairs

DESCRIPTION OF WORK

A number of lights are out in the back stairwell and basement because of what seem to be electrical issues. Someone has locked the storage unit from the inside and is living there. I know this has been a problem in the building before—I suspect it has something to do with the lights. I don't want to alarm the renters. Please send out maintenance with appropriate law enforcement for trespassing and arrest.

(Signature) _____
(Date) _____ 2.13.13 _____

SATURDAYS
AT HOME

Turn on the radio to NPR because as a human in the world living alone the voices are a comfort. Listen to Car Talk reruns and cry over the French Press because the show is no longer broadcast live and that's one way to measure time.

Go to the fridge and stand in front of it, door open, for a full ten unfocused minutes before pulling out the Sauvignon Blanc. Toast to dads everywhere: Thanks, Dad, for not being here to shout about energy wasted.

Call your father a little tipsy on Saturday afternoon. Tell him you left another man and receive your hearty congratulations. Tell him you have a broken heart and when he says, "again?" tell him you love him because the need to say something is strong.

Call the building manager when the light in your refrigerator burns out after leaving the door open all day. Tell her you can't find your wine. When she brings the tiny light bulb and sees the empty wine bottle on the counter and Saturday is in the best stretches of early evening, don't tell her you love her no matter how true.

To: Admin@metmgmt.net
Subject: Work Order Follow-Up
3/21/13

Work order about electrical issues in a series of lights in the back stairwell. Submitted this in January but am submitting a new one because the back staircase/basement lights have been dark for far too long.

ALL FIELDS MUST BE COMPLETED FOR CONSIDERATION OF APPROVAL BY MANAGEMENT

Building Name: Malden
Unit #: Back Stairs
Permission to Enter: ☒   Yes (quickest option)
              ☐   No (please schedule an appointment)
Pet(s):   ☐   Yes
      ☒   No
*If pets are present & maintenance cannot enter due to pets, a $75 administrative fee will be applied

☐   Priority 1 - Emergency! - No hot or cold water, heat or electricity, or a condition which is imminently hazardous to life

☒   Priority 2 - High Priority - Repair to a major appliance (range/oven, refrigerator) or a major plumbing issue

☐   Priority 3 - Standard repair - all other repairs

DESCRIPTION OF WORK

Electric issue—multiple lights in back staircase and the basement level not working. Looked for the fuse that may be causing this and could not find it. Found instead, frustration, rats, and raccoons. Please send someone out to determine what is wrong. This has been an issue for at least two months now. The rats, they grow aggressive.

(Signature) _____

(Date) _____3.21.13_____

ANIMAL CONTROL

The raccoon (*P. lotor*), also known as the common raccoon, mates for life.

It doesn't have to be dramatic. These two in the parking lot, preserved by the frigid air, had any number of lovers before each other. Had been in the getting-to-know-each-other-in-bed stages of getting to know each other. They hadn't had a proper fight even. They were keeping it casual, no expectation of dying together.

Social and argumentative, it is not uncommon for the raccoon, specifically the North American raccoon, to fight to the death in turf wars.

But these two, too round, too fresh, have no scratches, bites, or blood. They are not flattened, not distressed. They are not under any tires or close enough to, or to each other, to assume some sort of romance or vehicular slaughter.

Raccoons can also be spelled racoons, but gemination is more appropriate for an intransitive mating for life.

Neither forbidden nor forever—just two raccoons without expectations when they met at the edge of this parking lot two months ago. Last month, when the boar sliced his thumb open on a wine glass over dinner and the sow made sure he got home safe, they passed under the motion detector light in the parking lot. The injured boar limped and the sow stood ground in the illuminated lot, growling at the two humans smoking by the building, yards away. This was a sliver of sharing something besides the poison currently in their blood. That next morning, like any morning, each raccoon found breakfast on its own.

Signs of weakness, in all manner of vermin, are dangerous—in the city, in the forest, in the home.

Yesterday they feasted on fettuccine carbonara and the poison that killed them and the boar pointed out that, based on their urban lifestyle, they had, at most, one more year, given their life expectancy. "Oh?" The sow calculated her response, "Then if this ended now and we both live another year, we will have spent 5% of our lives together." "And if we die tomorrow, we've spent nearly 10%." "I've been thinking I'd like to have a kit," the sow slipped in, "no expectations."

The northern raccoon is not picky. There is no latch they cannot unlatch, no patch of urban unrest they cannot make a den.

The gravel in their fur now is just gravel, despite the number of times they groomed these same rocks from each other's coats after a romp in what leftovers the city has to give. The leftovers are just leftovers—dirty and delicious. The dirt between their toes; the dirt. The raccoons; unidentifiable from all other raccoons. This is their eulogy.

The service is a surprise party; this group gathered here smoking in the parking lot. The hope was to take care of the rats. A big haul, these lovers are large and no one is willing to determine if they are fifteen pounds or less, much less double bag them and throw them away. They look to be 25 pounds, 40. Urbanized raccoons can reach up to 60 pounds, two combined at 120. One woman says, *I'm 120*, and an older man nods, an authority, apparently.

The original coonskin cap consisted of the entire raccoon including its head and tail. An art all but lost and a fashion accessory all but unnecessary in the city.

No one wants a new hat so the building manager calls the city. The city dispatches animal control and they arrive with industrial gloves, coveralls, and galoshes. They carry spears the length of any arm that might have wrapped around a shoulder and celebrated in solidarity at this double murder, this fight to the death between man and *Procyon lotor*. The city spears the raccoons into the boxes they will burn in.

Raccoons don't mate for life. I made that up to make you think this story is about someone else.

To: Admin@metmgmt.net
Subject: Work Order Follow-Up
4/3/13

Followed up with another work order for this issue last month (or the month before?)

ALL FIELDS MUST BE COMPLETED FOR CONSIDERATION OF APPROVAL BY MANAGEMENT

Building Name: Malden
Unit #: Back Stairs
Permission to Enter: ☒ Yes (quickest option)
 ☐ No (please schedule an appointment)
Pet(s): ☐ Yes
 ☒ No
*If pets are present & maintenance cannot enter due to pets, a $75 administrative fee will be applied

 ☐ Priority 1 - Emergency! - No hot or cold water, heat or electricity, or a condition which is imminently hazardous to life

 ☒ Priority 2 - High Priority - Repair to a major appliance (range/oven, refrigerator) or a major plumbing issue

 ☐ Priority 3 - Standard repair - all other repairs

DESCRIPTION OF WORK

Lights have been out in the back stairwell for months now. If it isn't an electrical problem and it's just a fuse I will feel stupid, but I can't find the burnt out fuse and the lights have been out since… forever? During this forever I heard a young boy express fear holding his mother's hand, climbing the darkened stairs. "I'm scared," he said. Can't you see we're frightened?

(Signature) _____
(Date) _____ 4.3.13 _____

NOTES ON MAINTENANCE

It's enough to wake up and find the shower already used—the PVC liner holding droplets in its creases, the soap scum more scummy. It's enough to find not everything as it was when she locked the door and cocooned in her comforter—the razor at a different angle in the bath caddy, the books no longer stacked to size.

Because her roommate is messy she thinks it must be a man. A petite man because he must have borrowed her best black jeans because where else could they have gone? He never borrowed her clothes before, but he never lived here before.

She never sees him and isn't sure where he sleeps. In the one bedroom, there's only her bed, and the couch is never disturbed in the morning. Yet, the toilet roll needs replacing and the toothpaste has been squeezed from the top. She surveys room after room and leaves notes behind her.

Finding a couple half-full beers on the kitchen counter she sticks a note on the fridge, *Your beer bottles attract flies*; a travel-size shampoo in the shower, she sticks a note above the towel rack, *Please clean the tub*; Her pants still missing, she tapes a note on the light switch near the bedroom door, *Give me my pants back*.

Finding his foreign toothbrush in her cabinet, at least he is not using hers, but she wishes he would contribute to some utilities. And if the company finds out he is living here, he's not on the lease and she doesn't even know his name.

Waking late, alone, she finds herself in need of a shower and takes the time to *clean the tub*. She goes to the kitchen and throws the window open hoping the fruit flies will choose to stay so she can tell herself, at least I can *attract flies*. She empties the beer bottles and heads to the bedroom to get dressed and finds her *pants back* behind the bedframe. Clothed, she deals with the recycling. It is enough to find all the mess only her own.

THREE-DAY NOTICE TO PAY OR VACATE
XXXXXXXXXXXX XXXXXXXXXX Co.
P.O. BOX XXXXX
SEATTLE, WA 981XX

Date: 04/11/13
From: Property Manager / Agent for Owner
To: XXXX XXXXXX, et al.
XXXX E Harrison St Apt 201
Seattle, WA 981XX

Dear XXXX XXXXXX, et. al:
You and each of you are hereby notified and informed that rent for the period below for premises situated at the above address and county is now due and payable in the following amount:

TOTAL AMOUNT DUE NOW:

$1,315 Rent + $150 Late Fee =$1465

I had a job. I waited tables at a shitty sports bar in the stadium district. I was a shitty waitress so it was a good fit. The bar was swarmed on game days and lifting a wallet or two was easy as getting laid and more profitable. The first time a man left money on my nightstand he called me by my real name. "Goodbye," he said. It was twenty bucks.

I was fired for stealing an employee's lipstick. I was on my way to a date with a BHM who wanted me fresh from work for the grease smell. A splosher. I look at most men and think: if I dated them I would get fat. Just let myself go. Not because they would buy me extravagant meals, but because they are slobs. The trick is balancing multiple slobs and making them each feel special. This is simple when you are HWP and acting interested.

You are hereby notified and required to pay the above amount in full to the undersigned or his agent named below within three (3) days from the date of service of this notice upon you, or in the alternative, to vacate and surrender the premises.

I never host. Better to be able to leave than to have to wash someone out of your sheets. Everyone is betting their day's pocket change on yearning—taking the gamble of taking their pants off in front of another person. Betting the quarters that fall as they shed their clothes, that the other person won't just get up and leave. I'm gambling on the pocket change hitting the floor so I can use it to take the bus home while they sleep.

Domming is considered more lucrative than subbing. It's not untrue if you are a sub for someone into ageplay looking for a live-in daddy's girl. But find the man who uses misc. romance to post a photo of a mountain range alongside his newly penned poem about how society privileges action over contemplation, and you've found yourself a man who doesn't even know they're a sub. They'll think they're in love. What could be more submissive than that?

Give me a sap or a psychopath just so long as they give me the grace I need to make my rent. The desperate poet, the casual men looking for someone to play Strip Mario Brothers with, the ANR-seekers of the fetish world, even the NSA advertiser throws me cash for my cat's surgery, or a cab, if I spend enough time crying naked in their bed. I don't have a cat. I walk home.

In the event of; your failure to do so within the stated period, you will be guilty of unlawful detainer and subject to eviction as provided by law.

The building manager sends a follow-up email forty-eight hours after posting an eviction notice on my door. *This is serious*, she writes. *Also, you sent me a naked photo of yourself in an email. Just FYI.*

You too!? I respond. I write, *My boyfriend and I had a fight and he sent this photo to all my contacts. I'm so sorry!* I'm not sorry. Maybe the manager paused and contemplated if I was making her an offer. Maybe she imagined I was selling my body on Craigslist to make the rent and sent the email to her by accident. Or that I was selling my body on Craigslist to make the rent and sent her the photo so she would feel responsible. And what part of this would not be true?

After four dates with a 50-year-old m4w looking for a *Real Woman for Pretty Woman Role Play*, I spend the night. This is the plot point where I bag the wealthy Gere character. I tell him I'll be his wet nurse, his binky, that I'm willing to be trained. And we fall asleep like that, me lying into his ear, he lying in my arms. This man who described himself as a fan of *culturally astute ladies*, is not in the bed with me in the morning.

My things are hitting the curb across town. I want it to be dramatic but I'm sure it's mostly paperwork and a truck from the Goodwill arranged for pick-up. I imagine the scene as it should be—my clothes flying out the window into an open and waiting dumpster; the gift box in this man's living room waiting with new, respectable clothes for my new, respectable life with Richard Gere. I get out of bed and my clothes are missing. I enter the living room wrapped in his white sheet. Here is this man—the one whose ad specified that, *YOU: Can spell, use complete sentences*—bringing in the laundry.

I watch him sort my socks from his and fold them tight into each other.

By _____
Property Manager / Agent for Owner

Date notice was: 04/11/13
[___] hand delivered,
[_X_] mailed, and/or
[_X_] posted on APT: Apt: 201 door

APPROPRIATE FINERY

The man makes a home in the woman's storage space. After changing the lock and making his own key, he sneaks his only shirt and soiled pants into the wash of someone else's load. To cover himself while waiting for his clothes to clean, he wiggles his way into the only attire available. The dress is a comfort pressed hard to his skin, something with a little give at the seams, something unlike pavement.

He purges. Selling items for a meal and some smokes, he makes room for interior decoration. The rectangle of a comforter frames a sleeping bag bed. The armchair is angled in a corner, empty picture frames propped along the wall behind it. The humidifier he fills with water from the laundry room sink and goes about letting mold grow in the poorly ventilated space to keep the air damp and warm next to the bed. The man has things to take care of.

He unpacks the suitcase full of gowns slowly. He pulls out dress by dress to finger their loose seams and slipping hems. They imply a woman who has so much and cares for so little. He brings the fabrics to his face, sniffing out the sweat stains of ownership. He studies the shapes her odor has patterned; the way it radiates away from the armpits of her dresses becomes familiar.

He fills the empty clothes, layering dress after dress onto his too-large self, wishing for a day when he'll have a person to play dress up with rather than playing dress up with a person's life. He sees she is a smoker from the cigarette shaped hole in the folds of a skirt. She must be a little wild based on the rip up the back seam on more than one dress. She doesn't dry clean. She doesn't sew. He knows she is petite as he takes pleasure in the quiet splitting of stitches under his armpits. His tears will blend with hers and his perspiration will dilute hers and, in this way, he can inhabit her.

One day he hears footsteps on the cement floor of the basement hallway stop in front of his door. He hopes it's her, the woman whose dresses he wears. Then there's silence buoyed by the evaporating water from the humidifier. It sighs steam and gurgles. The man sits in the armchair, expectant, hoping for company, fit to entertain.

She is walking home when a man, bulging out of her vintage green dress, walks by. She knows it is her vintage green dress because of the circles under the armpits, the drooping hem, and the long-dried beer drip over the left torso panel, so crass on silk. It's embarrassing.

The man doesn't notice her as he enters the back of her apartment building. The woman gathers up her embarrassment and heads to the basement, but her key will not open the lock to her storage space.

She prepares to knock but hesitation waves her hand away. The woman doubts if she's in the right building, if she's paid her rent, if by neglecting her dress she's lost the shape she needs to get back into it. She thinks, removed the dress isn't fine. It is only fine in the wearing of it. She decides to be glad. It's appropriate, she thinks, that there's some life taking place beneath that fraying collar.

To: Admin@metmgmt.net
Subject: Work Order Follow-Up
4/21/13

This is the third (?) time I'm submitting a work order about the back stairs lighting issues.

ALL FIELDS MUST BE COMPLETED FOR CONSIDERATION OF APPROVAL BY MANAGEMENT

Building Name: Malden
Unit #: Back Stairs
Permission to Enter:　　**X**　Yes (quickest option)
　　　　　　　　　　　　　□　No (please schedule an appointment)
Pet(s):　　□　Yes
　　　　　　X　No
*If pets are present & maintenance cannot enter due to pets, a $75 administrative fee will be applied

X　Priority 1 - Emergency! - No hot or cold water, heat or electricity, or a condition which is imminently hazardous to life

□　Priority 2 - High Priority - Repair to a major appliance (range/oven, refrigerator) or a major plumbing issue

□　Priority 3 - Standard repair - all other repairs

DESCRIPTION OF WORK

The back staircase seems to have an electrical issue. The light between the first and second floor, and the basement lights are out. We resorted to wearing days-old underwear due the overwhelming creep factor of the laundry room. The building began to reek of us and the pheromones drove the dogs wild. They have taken hold of the back stairs and will not allow entry to the basement or back alley. At night you can hear the rats in the boiler room being hunted. No apparent burnt-out fuses in the building. Please send someone to check and fix the wiring. We are trapped.

(Signature) _____

(Date) _____4.21.13_____

ANY OLD
APOCALYPSE

There is a clog in the pipe in the ceiling. This explains the leak from the pipe in the space between the floor above and the ceiling above the bathtub. The pipe, soft and corroded, bubbles the ceiling and gathers in the basin for bathing. Maintenance doesn't have the snake they need to clear the clog. When the boxed-in claw foot can no longer contain the leak and it puddles in the indents of one hundred years of footsteps, shuffles, knees and backs pressed into the wood-warped floor, no one minds. It means the clog is still in the pipe demanding overflow, off-site retainers, and buckets and buckets for catching all the leaking resulting from that space filled.

As the floor expands and the walls push away and someone enters the apartment and notices their ankles are wet and the second story collapses into the first story and the leak waterfalls, no one minds. There will be casualties.

When the water level is high enough to encounter the pipe of its source and the water bubbles and gurgles at the point of leakage, everyone thinks it's cute. When it goes silent as the pipe is submerged, the building filling to the top, everyone is placing bets on how it will end. When the nails bend out and the sealant peels away and the bricks dissolve and the glass shatters under the pressure of the water and the pressure of their square frames forced trapezoidal, then the dam of the building breaks and the water from the leak from the clog stops eking out from under the front door and looses a radial tidal. The winners do not collect on the bets, everyone wrong is underwater.

When the tide finds its edge for a moment of calm and the leak goes on leaking from the pipe exposed now, it offers something to look up to from the edges of the lake the leak has claimed. These depths change every day and the stakes rise in the gambling culture everyone now lives in. The losers find their pets drowned, the photographs and artifacts of their memories consumed. The winners ban bridges from floating across the increasing leak-made lake so that every inch of shore is accessible to the expansion.

The winners become shipbuilders, deep-water divers, historians of this new era, archiving what is lost under the surface of this sea steady rising. There is a new math, a new measurement of time and distance. This is the era of post-clog and present leak, this is the age of all-in and nothing to lose. The casualties become something to wager and everyone is gambling with their lives. There are no docks to aim for; the shape-shifting body of the leak lake leaking negates navigation.

The ships in this leak are unmoored, preferring horizon's horrifying endlessness. Their hulls displace the volume of this uncharted mess, ever leaking, ever clogged. Every liter of lake, of waking lake waters, drown the solid world and the soil is easily boarded, undeveloped as it was.

It's the clogging that pipe in that building creating the leak at the center of this lake with these boats on it. And it's the boats, S.S. Everyman, so heavy in this lake that rises and rises in reaction and in reaction the shore is taken under and the tides of this simple shifting tsunami are rushing to the foothills of the cascades and slapping against cliffs and clapping the continent into islands, snow-capped peaks protruding.

Still the dripping gathering, dispersing, dripping, defying determined systems of measurement. Still the wagering of winners, only winners left at the end of everything with no end in sight. It doesn't take long to lose the memory of the clog in the pipe, the pipe that is leaking, the leaking that was a lake, a sea, an eddy and is now the vast and pulsing ocean. No one needs to remember the source of all this water to accept the waves and for the waves to crest in time with their source. No one can tell where the clog is still under all these areas flooded and under all these ships pushed out to open water. It is just so and all that is known.

ACKNOWLEDGMENTS

Seth and Bryan, you amaze me. Thanks to the editors and staff of the following publications for publishing portions of *Adventures in Property Management*: *Sonora Review* for publishing "Every Arrangement" and to Matt Bell for selecting the story as second runner-up for their Short Fiction Contest. *Everyday Genius* and guest editor Mark Cugini for publishing "Animal Control." *Cream City Review* for publishing "Appropriate Finery," *Monkeybicycle* for publishing "Housebroken," *Psychopomp Magazine* for publishing "Any Old Apocalypse," and *Queen Mob's Tea House* for publishing "Work Order Request Form" as a series. Thank you also to the Ragdale Foundation for the residency during which *Adventures in Property Management* took shape. Special thanks to my family for all their support and love and to Anna Balint for encouraging me to focus on apartment stories. Joe Rudko, Shaun Kardinal, Daniel Carillo, you guys make me look good. To Metropolitan Management, thanks for the job while it lasted.

ABOUT THE AUTHOR

Chelsea Werner-Jatzke is the author of *Thunder Lizard (Dinosauria, Sauropoda)* (H_NGM_N, 2016). She is the managing fiction editor at Pacifica Literary Review, editorial director at *Conium Review*, and co-founder of Till, an annual writing residency at Smoke Farm in Arlington, Washington. She has received support from Jack Straw Cultural Center as a writing fellow, from Artist Trust as an EDGE participant, and from the Cornish College Arts Incubator. She's received writing residencies from Vermont Studio Center and Ragdale Foundation. Werner-Jatzke has taught creative writing through Seattle Central Community College and served on the board of Lit Crawl Seattle. She received her MFA from Goddard College.

ABOUT
THE PRESS

Sibling Rivalry Press is an independent press based in Little Rock, Arkansas. It is a sponsored project of Fractured Atlas, a nonprofit arts service organization. Contributions to support the operations of Sibling Rivalry Press are tax-deductible to the extent permitted by law, and your donations will directly assist in the publication of work that disturbs and enraptures. To contribute to the publication of more books like this one, please visit our website and click *donate*.

Sibling Rivalry Press gratefully acknowledges the following donors, without whom this book would not be possible:

TJ Acena	JP Howard	Tina Parker
Kaveh Akbar	Shane Khosropour	Brody Parrish Craig
John-Michael Albert	Randy Kitchens	Patrick Pink
Kazim Ali	Jørgen Lien	Dennis Rhodes
Seth Eli Barlow	Stein Ove Lien	Paul Romero
Virginia Bell	Sandy Longhorn	Robert Siek
Ellie Black	Ed Madden	Scott Siler
Laure-Anne Bosselaar	Jessica Manack	Alana Smoot Samuelson
Dustin Brookshire	Sam & Mark Manivong	Loria Taylor
Alessandro Brusa	Thomas March	Hugh Tipping
Jessie Carty	Telly McGaha & Justin Brown	Alex J. Tunney
Philip F. Clark	Donnelle McGee	Ray Warman & Dan Kiser
Morell E. Mullins	David Meischen	Ben Westlie
Jonathan Forrest	Ron Mohring	Valerie Wetlaufer
Hal Gonzlaes	Laura Mullen	Nicholas Wong
Diane Greene	Eric Nguyen	Anonymous (18)
Brock Guthrie	David A. Nilsen	
Chris Herrmann	Joseph Osmundson	

www.ingramcontent.com/pod-product-compliance
Lightning Source LLC
Chambersburg PA
CBHW072020060426
42446CB00044B/3195